Scratch & Solve®
SPORTS HANGMAN

Mike Ward

**PUZZLE
WRIGHT
PRESS**

An imprint of Sterling
Publishing Co., Inc.

www.puzzlewright.com

Puzzlewright Press and the distinctive Puzzlewright Press logo are registered trademarks of Sterling Publishing Co., Inc.

Scratch & Solve is a registered trademark of Sterling Publishing Co., Inc.

18   20   19

Published by Sterling Publishing Co., Inc.
387 Park Avenue South, New York, NY 10016
© 2006 by Mike Ward, Brainteaser Publications
Distributed in Canada by Sterling Publishing
℅ Canadian Manda Group, 165 Dufferin Street
Toronto, Ontario, Canada M6K 3H6
Distributed in the United Kingdom by GMC Distribution Services
Castle Place, 166 High Street, Lewes, East Sussex, England BN7 1XU
Distributed in Australia by Capricorn Link (Australia) Pty. Ltd.
P.O. Box 704, Windsor, NSW 2756, Australia

Printed in China
All rights reserved

Sterling ISBN 978-1-4027-3721-3

For information about custom editions, special sales, premium and corporate purchases, please contact Sterling Special Sales Department at 800-805-5489 or specialsales@sterlingpublising.com.

How to Play Hangman

It's simple, easy, and great fun. You must fill in the missing letters at the bottom of each page before the body in the gallows is completed. Scratch the silver egg below one of the letters on the page. If you are correct, a number or more than one number will tell you where to enter this letter in the word or words below. If you are wrong, the hangman will stick his tongue out at you and you must fill in one of the dotted lines on the body in the gallows.

There are six parts to the body—two arms, two legs, a body, and the head. If you find all the letters in the complete word or phrase before you have to fill in six body parts, you win and the hangman will spare you. If not . . .

Good Luck!

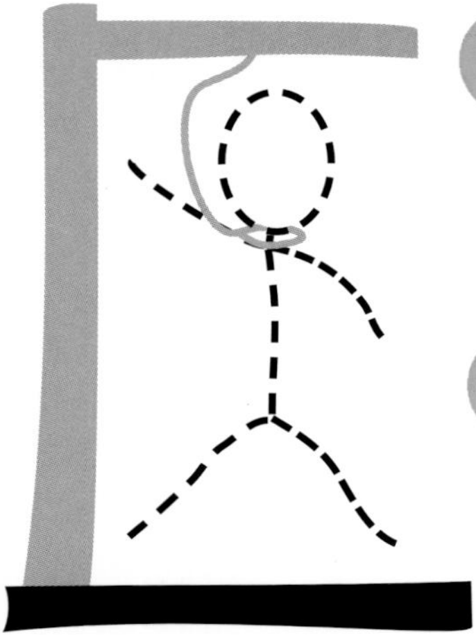

A   B   C   D   E   F   G

H   I   J   K   L   M

N   O   P   Q   R   S   T

U   V   W   X   Y   Z

4

$\overline{1}$ $\overline{2}$ $\overline{3}$ $\overline{4}$ $\overline{5}$ $\overline{6}$ $\overline{7}$ $\overline{8}$ $\overline{9}$

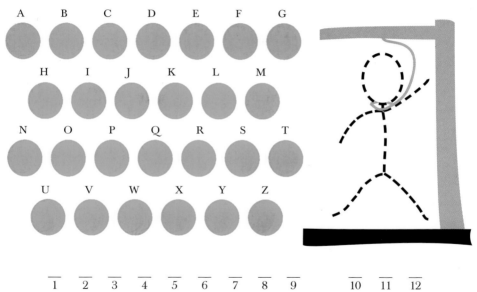

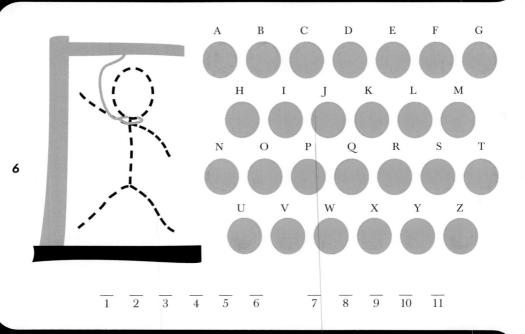

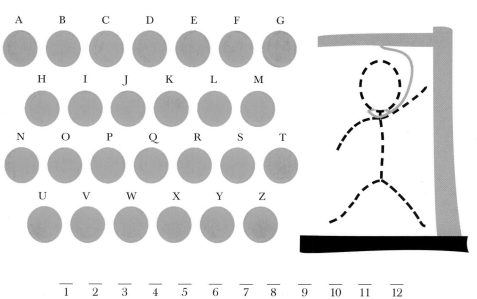

8

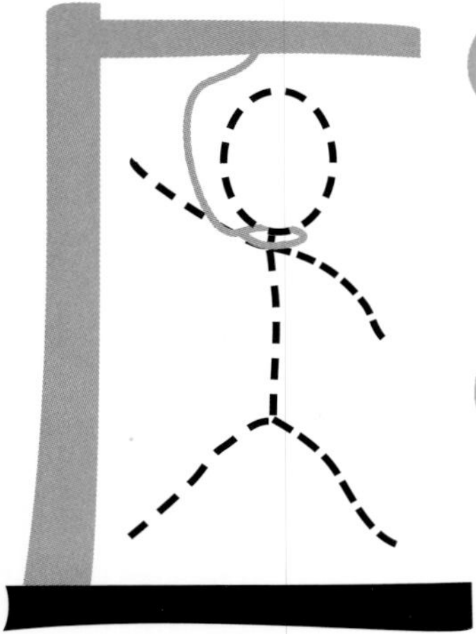

A B C D E F G

H I J K L M

N O P Q R S T

U V W X Y Z

$\overline{1}$ $\overline{2}$ $\overline{3}$ $\overline{4}$ $\overline{5}$ $\overline{6}$ $\overline{7}$ $\overline{8}$ $\overline{9}$ $\overline{10}$

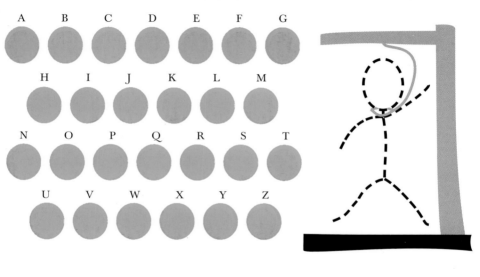

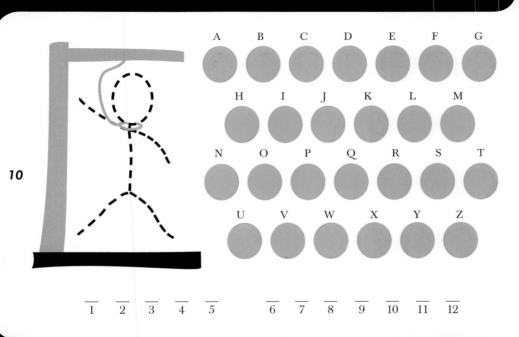

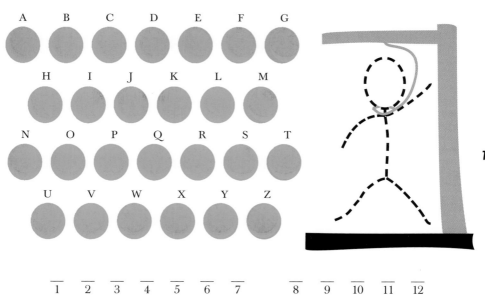

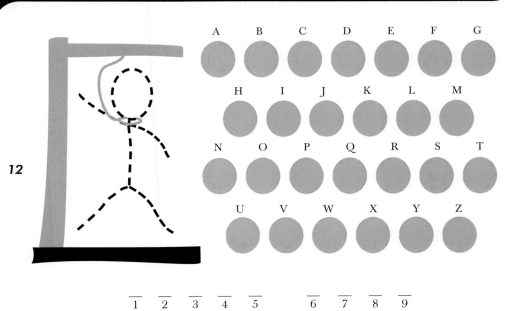

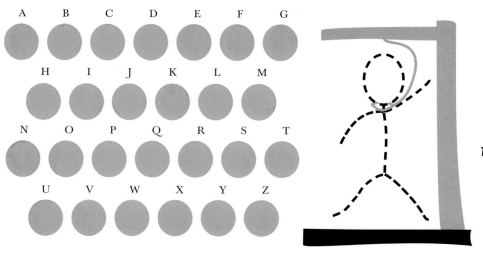

13

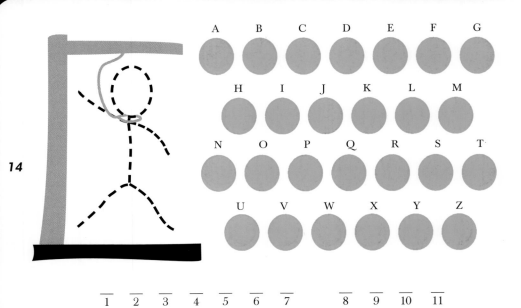

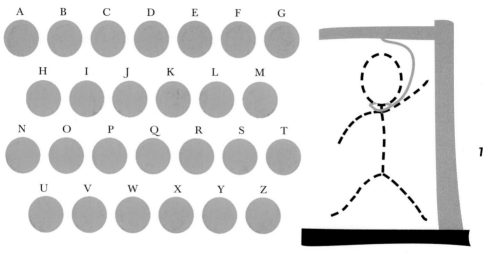

15

$\overline{1}$ $\overline{2}$ $\overline{3}$ $\overline{4}$ $\overline{5}$ $\overline{6}$ $\overline{7}$ $\overline{8}$ $\overline{9}$ $\overline{10}$ $\overline{11}$ $\overline{12}$ $\overline{13}$ $\overline{14}$

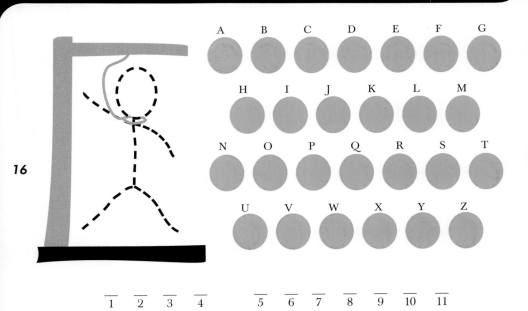

16

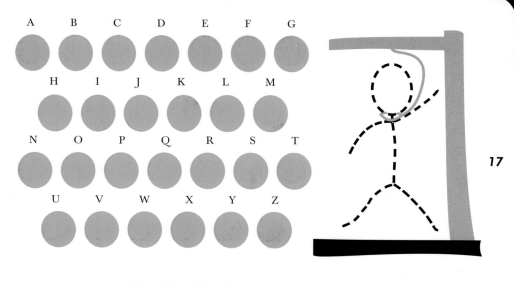

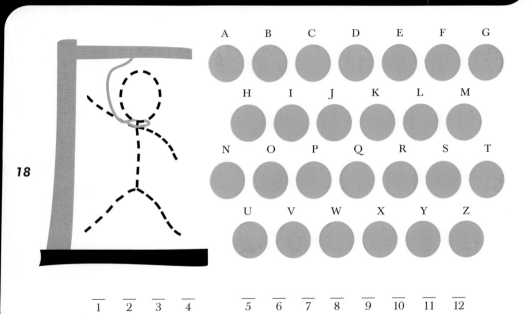

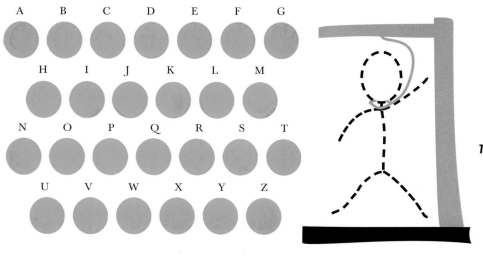

19

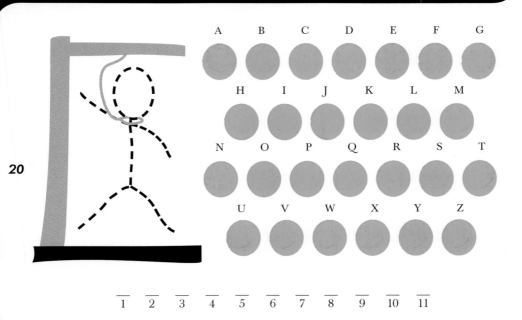

20

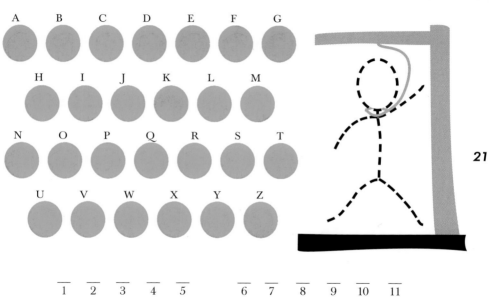

$\overline{}_1$ $\overline{}_2$ $\overline{}_3$ $\overline{}_4$ $\overline{}_5$ $\overline{}_6$ $\overline{}_7$ $\overline{}_8$ $\overline{}_9$ $\overline{}_{10}$ $\overline{}_{11}$

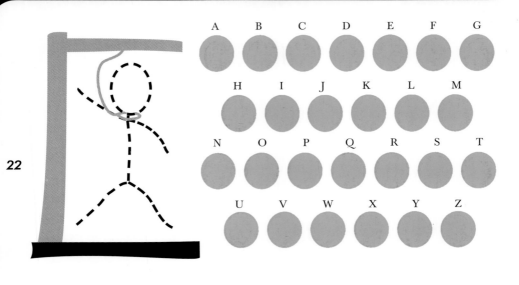

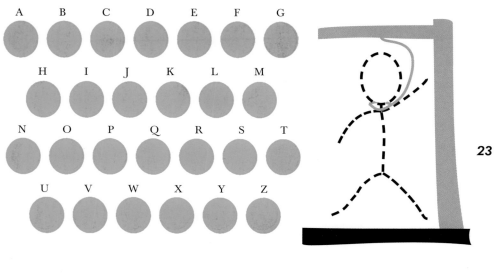

23

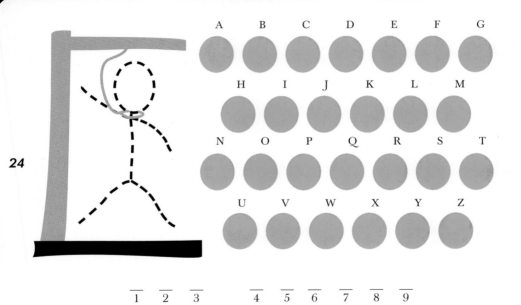

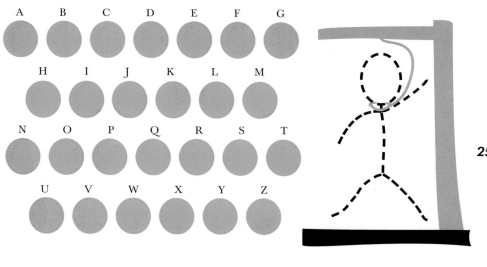

25

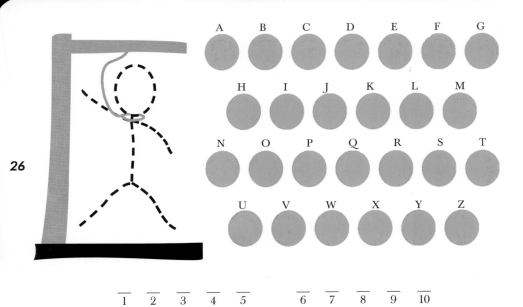

26

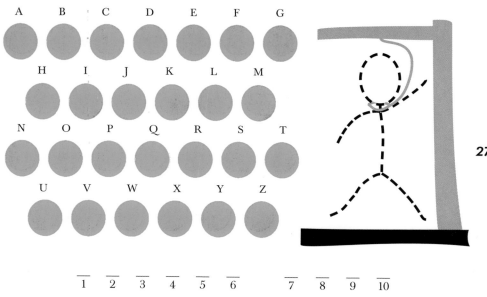

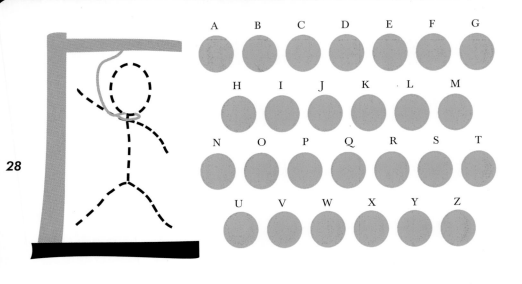

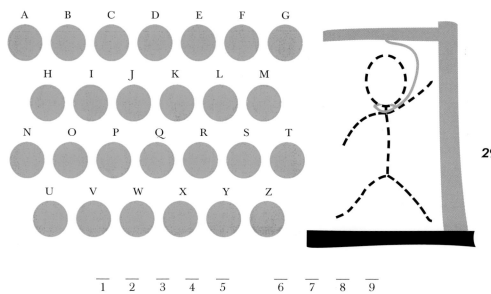

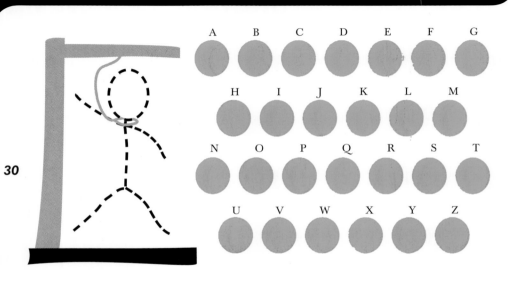

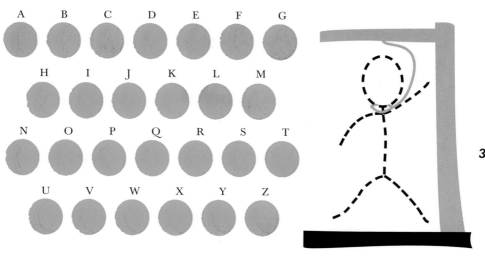

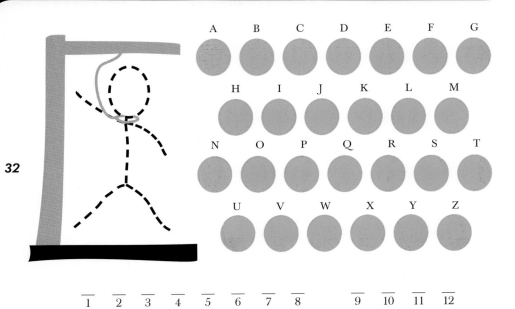

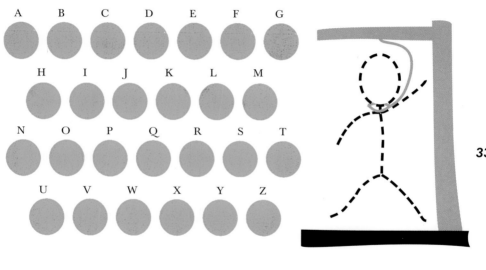

A B C D E F G
H I J K L M
N O P Q R S T
U V W X Y Z

$\overline{1}$ $\overline{2}$ $\overline{3}$ $\overline{4}$ $\quad$ $\overline{5}$ $\overline{6}$ $\overline{7}$ $\overline{8}$ $\overline{9}$

33

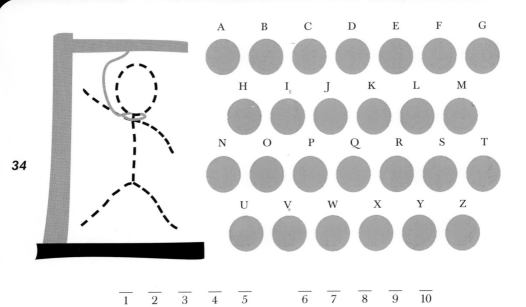

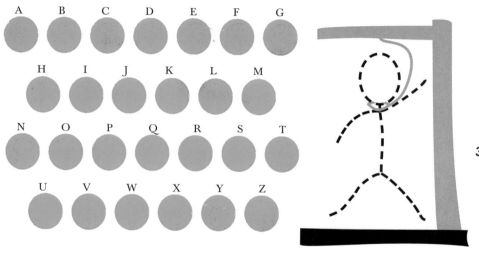

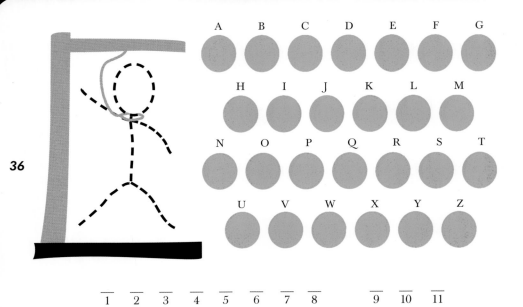

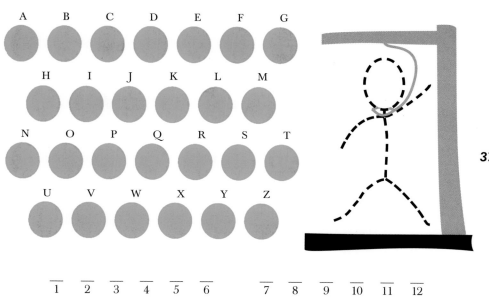

37

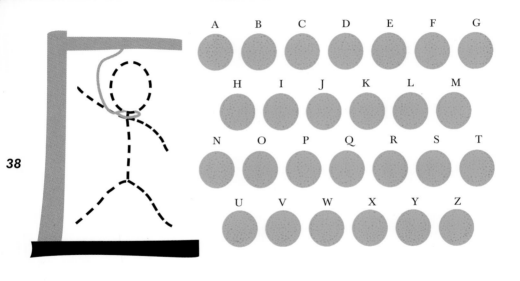

38

$\overline{}_1 \quad \overline{}_2 \quad \overline{}_3 \quad \overline{}_4 \quad \overline{}_5 \quad \overline{}_6 \quad \overline{}_7 \quad \overline{}_8 \quad \overline{}_9$

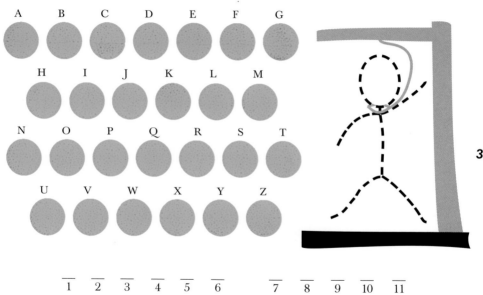

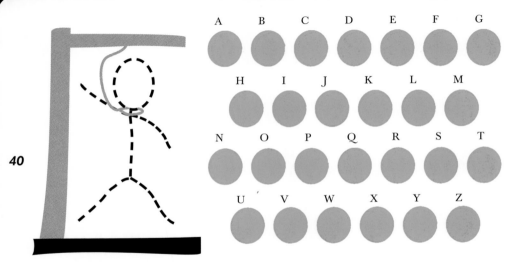

40

A   B   C   D   E   F   G

H   I   J   K   L   M

N   O   P   Q   R   S   T

U   V   W   X   Y   Z

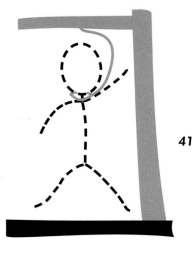

$\overline{1}$ $\overline{2}$ $\overline{3}$ $\overline{4}$ $\overline{5}$ $\overline{6}$ $\overline{7}$ $\overline{8}$ $\overline{9}$ $\overline{10}$

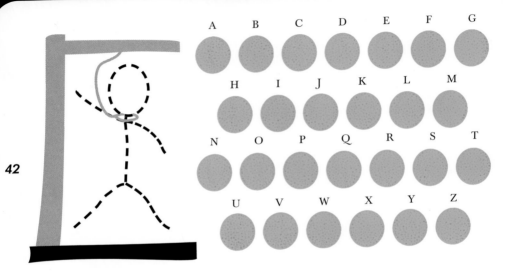

42

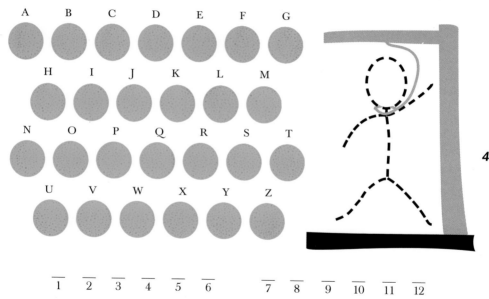

A   B   C   D   E   F   G

H   I   J   K   L   M

N   O   P   Q   R   S   T

U   V   W   X   Y   Z

$\overline{1}$ $\overline{2}$ $\overline{3}$ $\overline{4}$ $\overline{5}$ $\overline{6}$ $\overline{7}$ $\overline{8}$ $\overline{9}$ $\overline{10}$ $\overline{11}$ $\overline{12}$

43

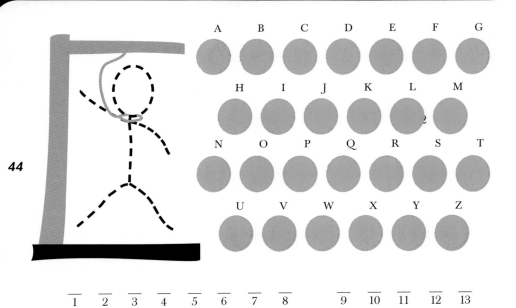

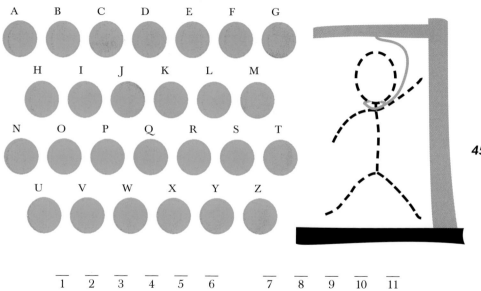

45

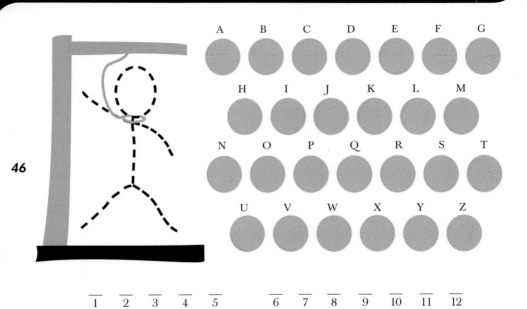

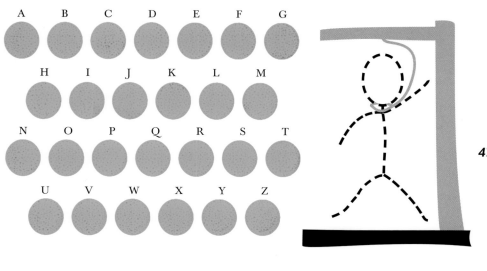

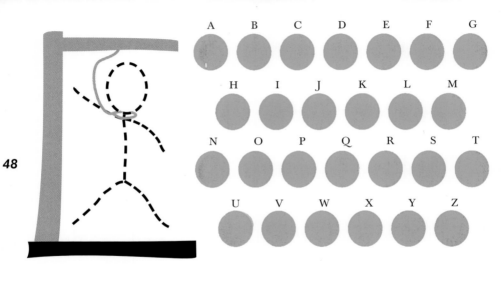

48

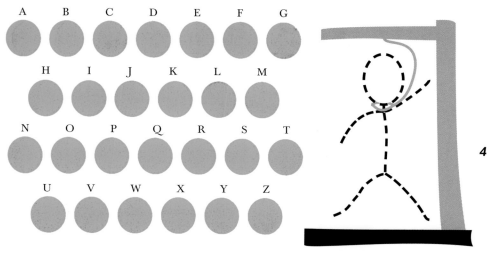

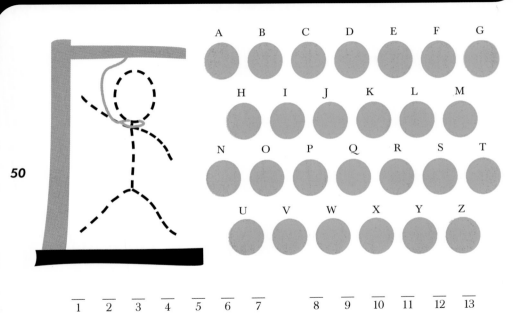

50

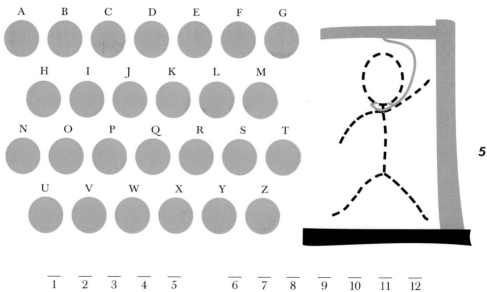

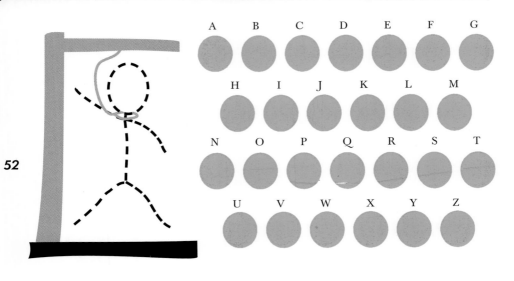

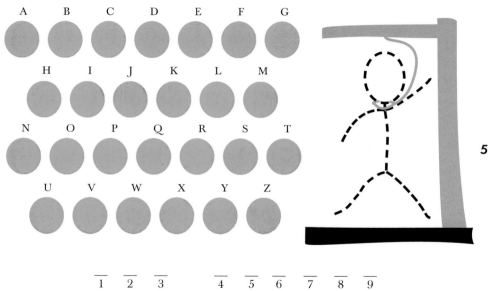

A B C D E F G

H I J K L M

N O P Q R S T

U V W X Y Z

$\overline{}$ $\overline{}$ $\overline{}$ $\overline{}$ $\overline{}$ $\overline{}$ $\overline{}$ $\overline{}$ $\overline{}$
1   2   3   4   5   6   7   8   9

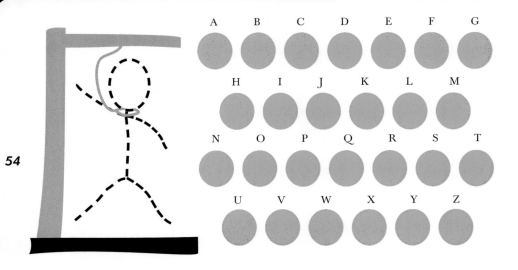

54

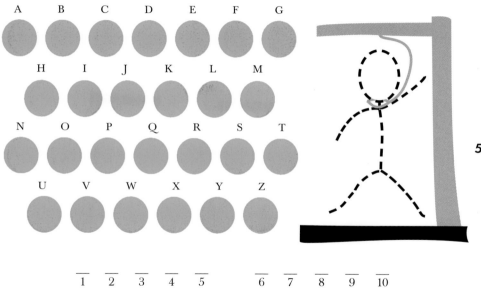

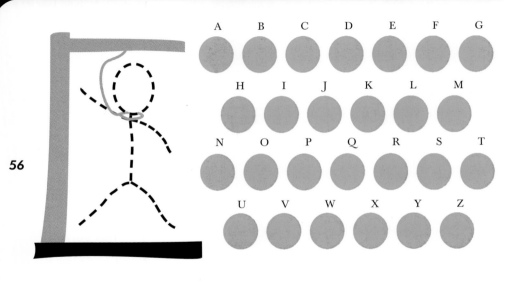

56

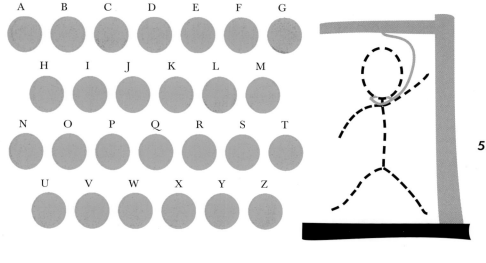

A B C D E F G

H I J K L M

N O P Q R S T

U V W X Y Z

$\overline{}$ $\overline{}$ $\overline{}$ $\overline{}$ $\quad$ $\overline{}$ $\overline{}$ $\overline{}$ $\overline{}$ $\overline{}$
1 2 3 4   5 6 7 8 9

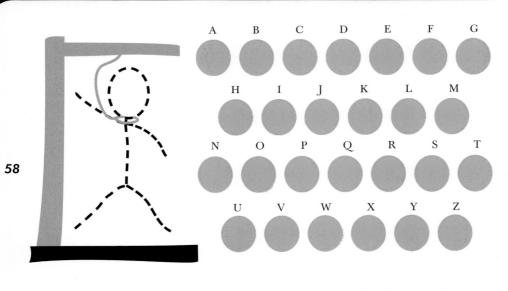

58

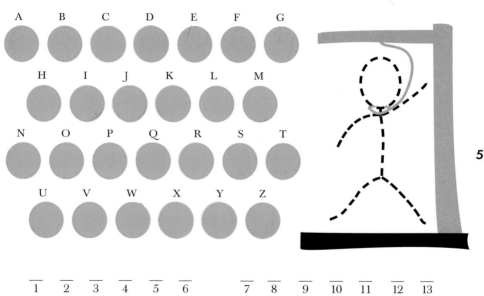

59

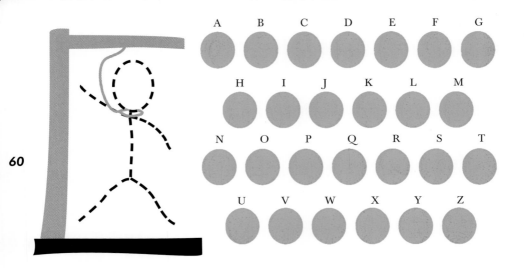

60

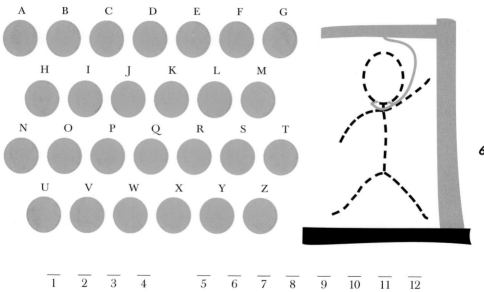

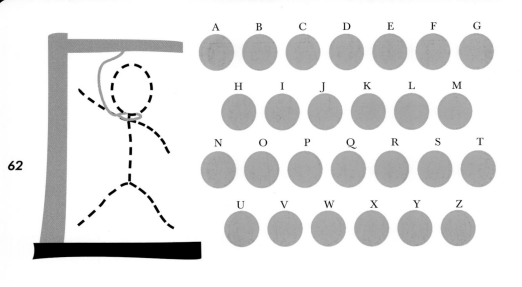

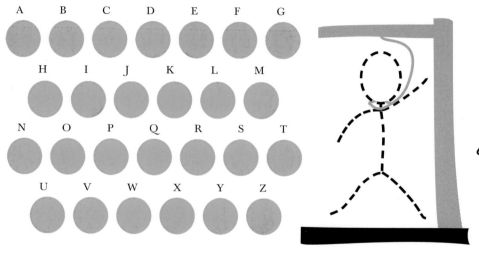

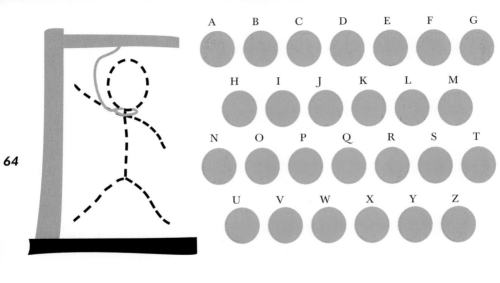

A B C D E F G

H I J K L M

N O P Q R S T

U V W X Y Z

$\overline{1}$ $\overline{2}$ $\overline{3}$ $\overline{4}$ $\overline{5}$ $\overline{6}$ $\overline{7}$ $\overline{8}$ $\overline{9}$ $\overline{10}$ $\overline{11}$ $\overline{12}$ $\overline{13}$

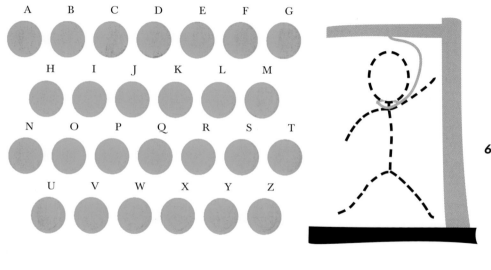

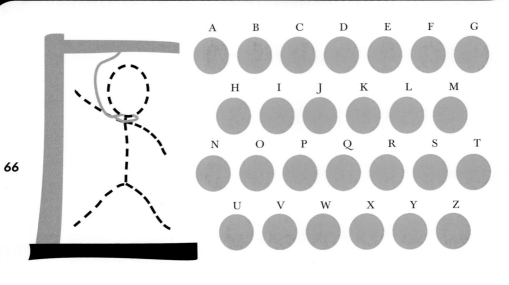

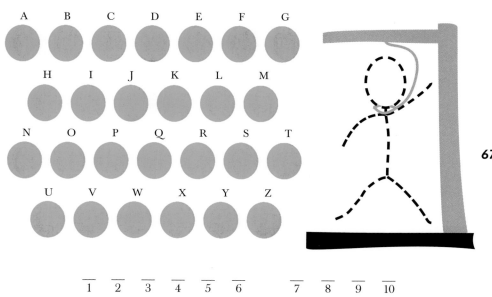

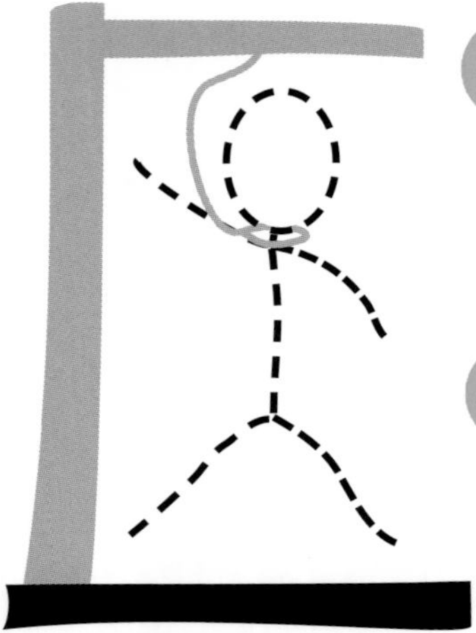

A B C D E F G
H I J K L M
N O P Q R S T
U V W X Y Z

$\overline{1}$ $\overline{2}$ $\overline{3}$ $\overline{4}$ $\overline{5}$ $\overline{6}$ $\overline{7}$ $\overline{8}$ $\overline{9}$ $\overline{10}$ $\overline{11}$

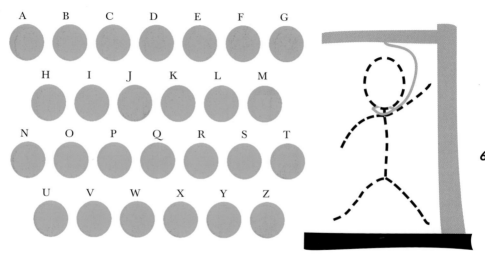

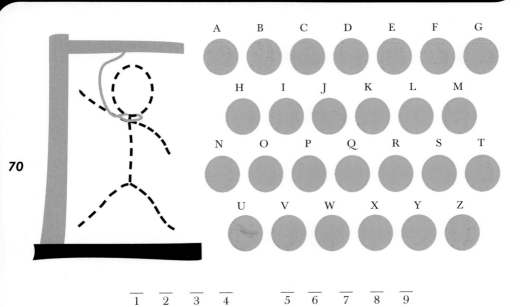

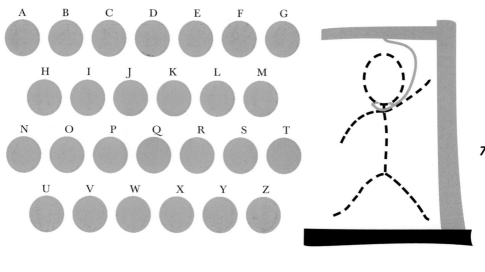

A B C D E F G

H I J K L M

N O P Q R S T

U V W X Y Z

$\overline{}$ $\overline{}$ $\overline{}$ $\overline{}$ $\overline{}$ $\overline{}$ $\overline{}$ $\overline{}$ $\overline{}$ $\overline{}$ $\overline{}$

1 2 3 4 5 6 7 8 9 10 11

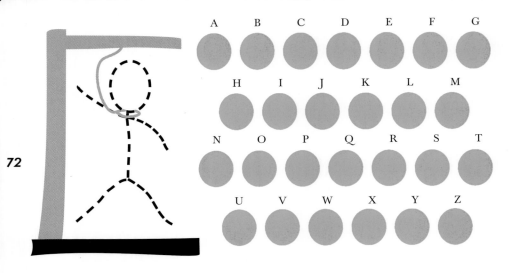

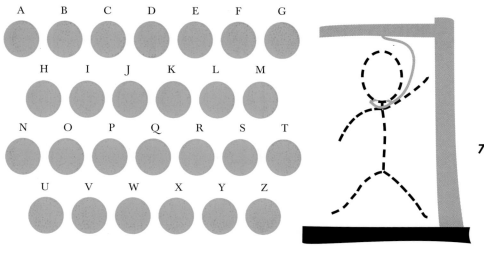

73

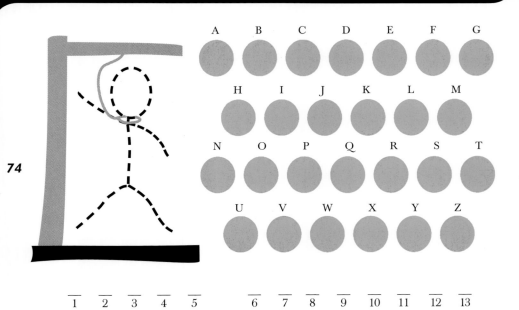

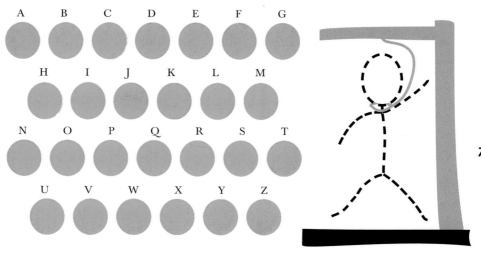

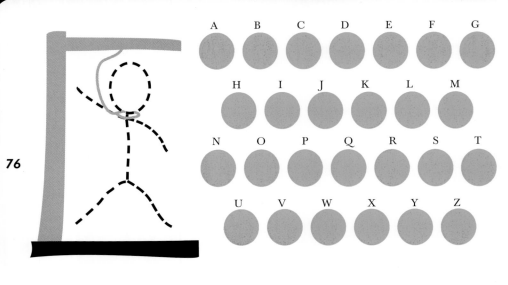

76

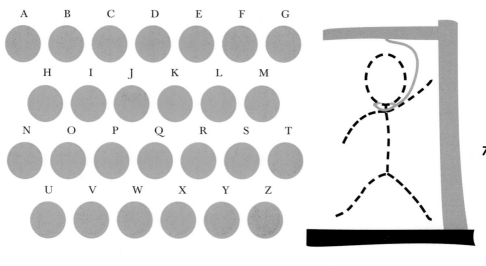

A B C D E F G

H I J K L M

N O P Q R S T

U V W X Y Z

$\overline{}$ $\overline{}$ $\overline{}$ $\overline{}$ $\overline{}$ $\overline{}$ $\overline{}$
1   2   3   4   5   6   7

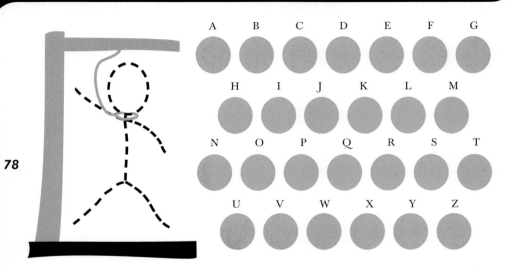

78

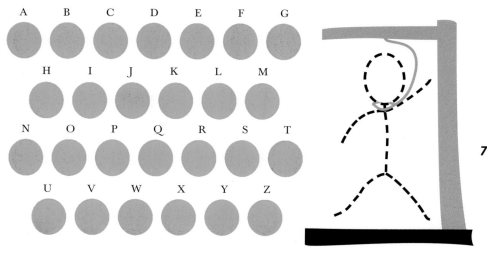

A   B   C   D   E   F   G

H   I   J   K   L   M

N   O   P   Q   R   S   T

U   V   W   X   Y   Z

$\overline{1}$ $\overline{2}$ $\overline{3}$ $\overline{4}$ $\overline{5}$ $\overline{6}$ $\overline{7}$ $\overline{8}$ $\overline{9}$ $\overline{10}$

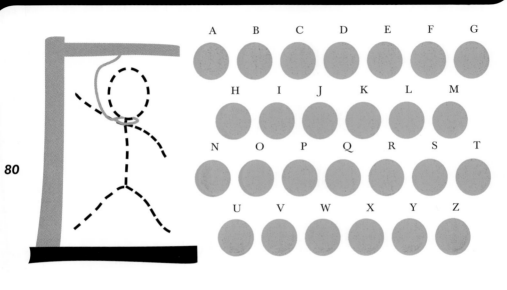

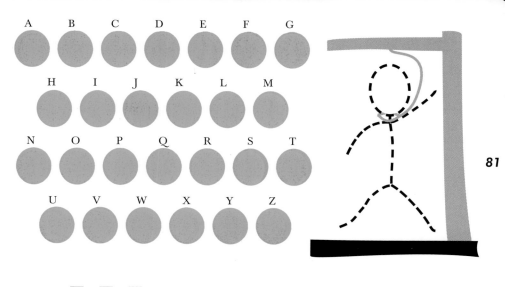

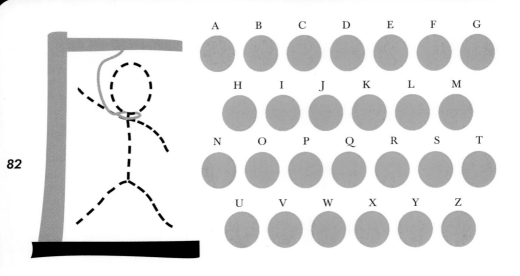

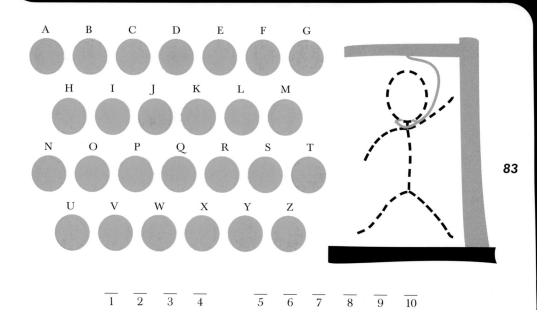

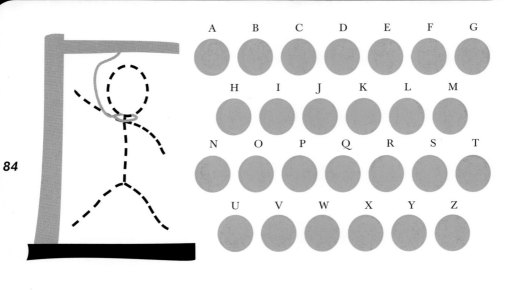

84

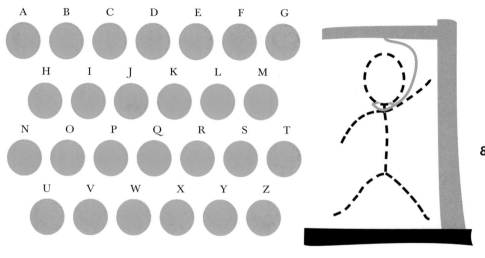

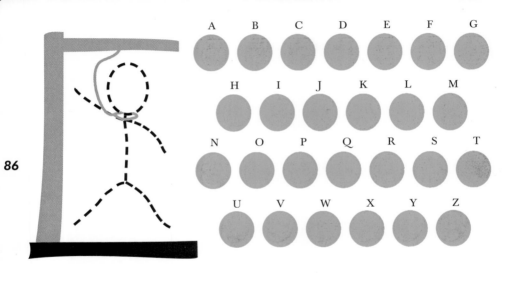

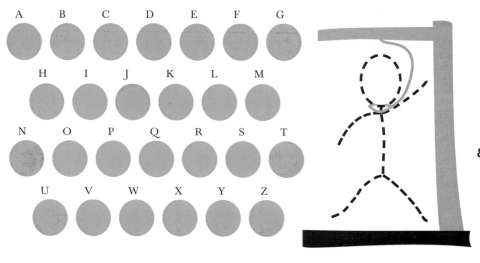

A B C D E F G

H I J K L M

N O P Q R S T

U V W X Y Z

$\overline{}$ $\overline{}$ $\overline{}$ $\overline{}$ $\overline{}$ $\overline{}$ $\overline{}$ $\overline{}$
1   2   3   4   5   6   7   8

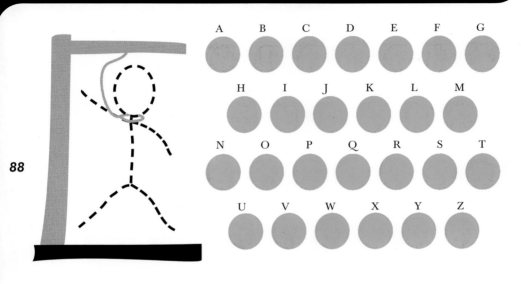

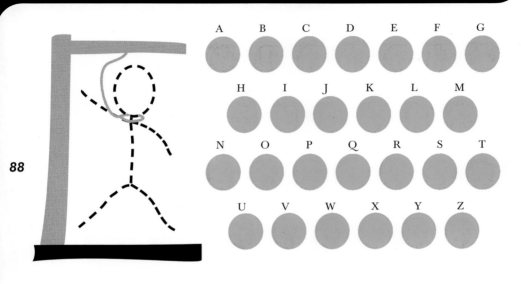

88

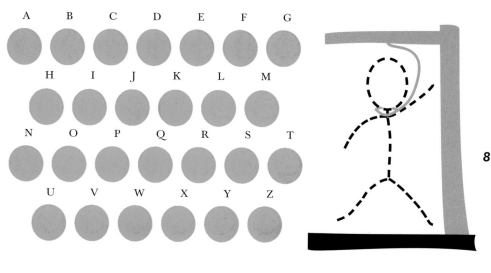

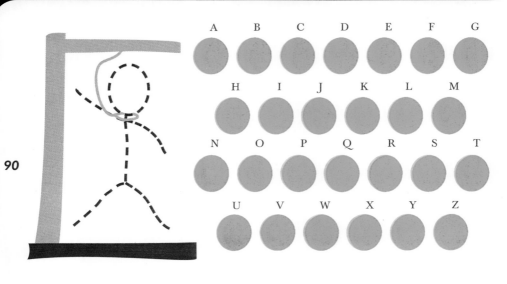

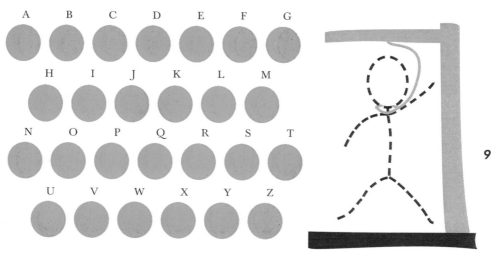

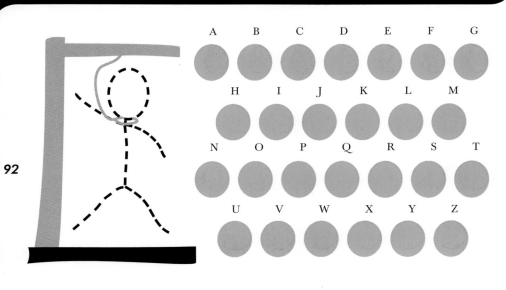

A   B   C   D   E   F   G

H   I   J   K   L   M

N   O   P   Q   R   S   T

U   V   W   X   Y   Z

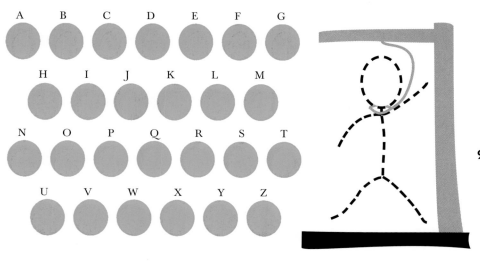

$\overline{}$ $\overline{}$ $\overline{}$ $\overline{}$ $\overline{}$ $\overline{}$ $\overline{}$ $\overline{}$
1   2   3   4   5   6   7   8

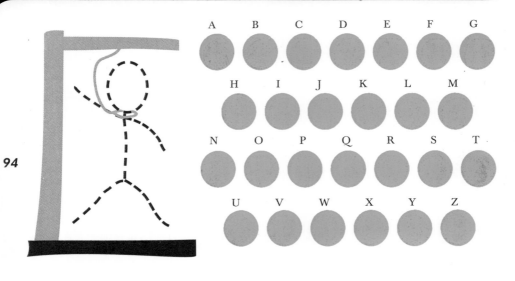